THE SECRET
to EFFECTIVE TITHES
and OFFERINGS

ARE YOUR GIFTS RESULTING IN BLESSINGS
FOR YOU AND THE RECEIVER?

by
TEDDY AND ELAINE PLEDGER

Copyright © 2014 by Teddy and Elaine Pledger

The Secret to Effective Tithes and Offerings
Are Your Gifts Resulting In Blessings For You And The Receiver?
by Teddy and Elaine Pledger

Printed in the United States of America

Edited by Xulon Press

ISBN 9781498422192

All rights reserved solely by the author. The author guarantees all contents are original and do not infringe upon the legal rights of any other person or work. No part of this book may be reproduced in any form without the permission of the author. The views expressed in this book are not necessarily those of the publisher.

Unless otherwise indicated, Scripture quotations are taken from the New American Standard Bible (NASB). Copyright © 1960, 1962, 1963, 1968, 1971, 1972, 1973, 1975, 1977, 1995 by The Lockman Foundation. Used by permission. All rights reserved.

www.xulonpress.com

Table of Contents

Introduction vii

Chapter 1: Are You Tithing And Giving To Be Prosperous? 11

Chapter 2: Is Your Faith For Prosperity In Your Tithes And Offerings? 19

Chapter 3: Are You Afraid To Not Tithe And Give? 25

Chapter 4: Are You Tithing And Giving With No Rejoicing? Are You Forced, Coerced, Or Feeling Guilty? Did You Give, Or Were You Taken? 29

Chapter 5: Are You in Agreement with Your Mate? 37

Chapter 6: Are You and Your Mate on Good Terms? 41

Chapter 7: Are You Meeting Your Family's Needs? 43

Chapter 8: Are You Tithing and Giving Instead of Paying Past-Due Bills? 49

Chapter 9:   Are You Giving Because You
             Saw A Need?..........................59

Chapter 10: Does Someone Have Something
             Against You?.........................67

Chapter 11: Do You Have Unforgiveness In
             Your Heart?..........................71

Chapter 12: Are You Tithing and Giving Without
             Getting God's Instructions About
             Where it Should Go?..................77

*A Word To Ministers, Elders, Deacons, Board
Members, And Businessmen* 89

About The Authors 93

Introduction

It is important to realize that all Christians have been given gifts by the Holy Spirit (some call these "motive gifts"), and each of us is to serve according to His gifting. The purpose of this book is to encourage all Christians to be led by the Holy Spirit in their tithing and giving, but especially those called to the ministry of giving.

Several years ago, my wife and I were part of an intercessory prayer group. We were learning the various forms of praying, how to flow together in the Holy Spirit, and how to pray effectively for others. One night while we were with this group, the leader stopped praise and worship and said that the Holy Spirit had told her that some in the group were in serious financial trouble. She asked for a show of hands of those who needed prayer for their finances. *Every person* in the place, between eighty to one hundred people, raised their hands. Many of those people we knew very well, and we knew that many tithed and gave more than the tithe. To us, these brothers and sisters were not the average Christian. They were fully committed to Jesus, praying for others, tithing and giving, yet they were in need.

We began right then crying out to God to know why their tithing and giving was not being blessed as the Father had promised. This book is what the Father has revealed to us since that time.

We have asked several people what kind of response they would expect if their Spirit-filled church asked for a show of hands of those who were in financial need. Most agree that from 50 to 75 percent would likely raise their hands. However, in denominational churches, only 10 to 15 percent would be expected to raise their hands.

We asked the Father why the giving of so many is not working for them, especially when many of them give sacrificially, while apparently the giving of those in denominational churches is working for them. He told us that those whose tithing and giving was not working were those who were tithing and giving wrong. He told us that if we could just be in neutral when we give, He could bless our giving. However, He could not bless our giving if the giving was done wrong. If God blessed something we did that was wrong, then His blessing would be teaching us that what we did wrong was right. God said that He could not bless wrongdoing.

The Father is seeking sons and daughters that He can trust with the wealth of the world. He is looking for those who will funnel this wealth into His kingdom as He wills. I trust that as you read this book and study the Scriptures referenced that you will be set completely free to be led by the Holy Spirit in the giving of your tithes and offerings. When you give as He directs, your tithes and offerings will be blessed, the harvest will come, and nothing in heaven, on earth, or in hell can stop it, for He who promised is faithful.

CHAPTER 1

ARE YOU TITHING AND GIVING TO BE PROSPEROUS?

Let me ask you a few questions. Can being good, doing a lot of good works, or abstaining from doing evil things get us into heaven? Of course not. What good things can we do to gain eternal life? The answer—nothing! We receive eternal life, salvation, and a home in heaven by faith. There is nothing we can do to earn it. Can being a good Christian, working in church, or helping the poor result in us walking in divine health? Of course not. What good things can we do to get healed? The answer again is nothing. We receive healing by faith; Jesus took stripes on His body for our healing. There is nothing we can do to earn healing. We receive health and healing by trusting in what Jesus did for us on the cross.

However, if I asked what good things we can do to be prosperous, some would respond that we can tithe and give, and we can sow seed. But that is wrong. There is nothing we can do to earn prosperity either.

In 2 Corinthians 8:9, the Bible says,

> For you know the *grace* of our Lord Jesus Christ, that though He was rich, yet for your sake, He became poor, so that you through *His* poverty might become rich (emphasis added).

Notice, it does not say that we, through our tithing and giving, might become rich. Jesus took our sin, our sickness, and our poverty to the cross and exchanged them for salvation, healing, and prosperity, all of which we receive by faith, not by doing good works (really, these are "dead" works).

I have heard a few ministers say things like, "My prosperity does not depend on your giving; it depends on *my* giving." Wrong again! Prosperity depends on us receiving it by faith. When we try to obtain something that Jesus died to give us, it will not be successful, because these are dead works, works of the flesh. It makes His sacrifice and death on the cross of no effect. We trample on His blood and deny the free gifts He purchased for us on the cross. This is most offensive to Father God. Much of the teaching we have had in the past about tithing and giving is nothing more than religious works.

Have you been tithing and giving so that you can get more? Then this is part of the problem. We do not give to get; we give because we have already received.

In Matthew 10:8, Jesus gave His disciples instructions before He sent them out, saying,

> Heal the sick, raise the dead, cleanse the lepers, cast out demons. *Freely you received, freely give* (emphasis added).

The disciples had received, so they were instructed to give.

How many times in the Bible did Jesus receive an offering from the multitudes? Zero— none! Did Jesus ever give an offering to the masses? Yes, He did, feeding the five thousand in Matthew 14:13–21 and the four thousand in Matthew 15:29–39.

Did the disciples have money? The Bible indicates they did. In fact, they had so much money that when Judas stole from the money bag, no one missed it. In Matthew 19:23, when Jesus said it was hard for a rich man to enter the kingdom of heaven, the disciples were amazed *because they had money.*

At the feeding of the four thousand, Jesus told them to feed the people.

Matthew 15:33 says,

> And the disciples said to Him, 'Where would we get so many loaves in a desolate place to satisfy such a great multitude?'

They did not ask where they were going to get money; they wanted to know where they could go to buy the food. I believe they had enough money to buy food for four thousand men, not counting women and children.

We do not give to get God to give. God gives first. God says in Job 41:11,

> Who has given to me that I should repay him? Whatever is under the whole heaven is Mine.

Similarly, Romans 11:35 says,

> Or who has first given to Him that it might be paid back to him again?

And 2 Corinthians 9:10 says,

> Now *He who supplies* seed to the sower and bread for food, *will supply and multiply* your seed for sowing and increase the harvest of your righteousness (emphasis added).

God gives first; He gives seed to be sown.

Frankly, it appears that much of the church has this sowing and reaping backwards. We act like we have to sow before we can reap. Jesus says that He has already sown; we must first reap, and then we begin to sow from the seed He has given us. You see, if we sowed first, we would be entitled to part of the glory, and 1 Corinthians 1:29 says,

> No man may boast before God.

Jesus should get all the glory for everything that happens, and we should claim nothing.

We should ask God for discernment to recognize when He gives us seed to sow. We do not want to eat our seed for sowing. If we do, there will be no harvest. We should also ask God to show us when He is bringing in the harvest. We are convinced there have been many of us who have given away God's harvest. What farmer do you know who would plant, plant, and plant but never reap a harvest? Sometimes the Father must get frustrated with us when He tries to bring to us the harvest for which we have sowed and we keep giving it away. God wants to bless us and give us the desires of our hearts.

This lesson was taught to us through a young lady, a single mom, in New Orleans. She continually gave to the Lord, even instead of paying bills. She had learned the principle of giving out of your need. (This will work when God tells you to do this, and it will work when you give out of your need.) She had to be helped with her apartment rent several times. One time she came into a harvest. However, instead of paying her bills and rent, she gave almost all of the money back to the Lord. It was at this time that the Lord showed us that He wants us to gather the harvest when He brings it to us. He greatly desires to bless us and for us to have nice things.

If you have been tithing and giving in order to be prosperous, please do the following:

- Confess this to the Father and repent (repent means to change your mind).

- Tithing and giving to get, when you get right down to the foundation, is nothing more than trying to bribe God.

- He will not respond to this type of attitude or motive, nor will this type of giving result in you being blessed.

- After repenting, continue to tithe and give.

- Remember, God does not get the money. All He gets is our heart's attitude, our love, our gratitude, and our honor when we tithe and give.

CHAPTER 2
IS YOUR FAITH FOR PROSPERITY IN YOUR TITHES AND OFFERINGS?

A minister was preaching one night, and started with Mark 11:22. When he got to the end of that verse, it was as though he and the congregation disappeared and Jesus began to minister to us from the last four words of that verse. The last four words of Mark 11:22 state,

> Have faith in God.

Jesus said that whatever we have our faith in is our God. He said that if that god's name is not Jesus, then that god is a false god (idol) that He must destroy from our lives.

In the Old Testament, the law stated that there could be no other gods before Him. I suppose this indicates that they may have had other gods, but He had to be the first and biggest. However, in the New Testament, we are to have no other gods at all—ever.

For example, have you learned how to take authority over Satan and demons—the enemy—binding him, loosing things and people, speaking to things, and dispatching angels? Remember how when you were first learning of your authority in Jesus, that when you rebuked or bound, it worked? Has the time come in your life when you have bound, rebuked, and loosed, but nothing has happened? Ever ask yourself why?

My wife and I were in London, getting ready to return home. We packed our bags, blessed them, bound the devil, blessed the baggage handlers, and spoke to the bags. We did everything we knew to do to be sure that our bags arrived home with us. We went to the airport, checked in, boarded the plane, and then landed in New York to go through customs. However, our bags did not make it onto that one airplane to New York. There were no plane changes involved or anything else. Our bags just did not get on that one plane.

I was angry and greatly disappointed. I cried out to God, "What good does it do to have a God like You when we do everything You have taught us—we bound, rebuked, blessed, and spoke to the bags—and it did not work?" Three days later at home, still with no bags, I was walking down the sidewalk to pick up the mail when Jesus spoke to me and said, "Do you know why your bags did not arrive with you?" I said, "No, I've been asking You for three days why they were lost." He said, "The reason the bags got lost is because you had your faith in your little ritual instead of having your faith in Me. If your faith had been in Me, your bags would have arrived with you, both in New York and at home."

It is very important to know how to bind, loose, rebuke, bless, and speak to things so that when the Holy Spirit tells us to do these things, it will work every time. If we bind, rebuke, and so forth without His instructions to do so, it is a work of the flesh, and sooner or later it will not work. An example of this is in Acts 19:14 when the seven sons of Sceva were attempting to cast demons out of a possessed man. The man with the demons jumped on them, stripped and wounded them, and chased them away. Operating spiritual things in the flesh is dangerous.

It is important to make Bible confessions, say what God says, plead the blood of Jesus for protection, bind, rebuke, and loose. However, if our faith is ever placed in these things we say or do—our rituals—we will soon be in serious trouble. These things can become our gods, and then the true God must destroy those gods. Therefore, let us always examine ourselves to know that when we speak the things we've been taught, our real faith is in the Father, Jesus, and the Holy Spirit, not in what we say or do. We can have confidence that when we speak, led by the Spirit, things will happen, but our faith must be in God and nothing else.

Thus we see that if our faith for prosperity is in the fact that we tithe and give, our prosperity god is tithing and giving, not Father God, Jesus, or the Holy Spirit. Father God must then destroy and render useless or worthless our prosperity god. Remember, God will not bless something that is right if it is done for the wrong reason.

Actually, for tithing to work, it takes no faith. In Malachi 3:10, God says,

> Bring the whole tithe into the storehouse so that there may be food in My house, and *test Me now in this,*' says the Lord of hosts, 'if I will not open for you the windows of heaven, and pour out for you a blessing until it overflows (emphasis added).

If we have to test God, it means that we have no faith that He will do as He said. This invitation to test God is the only place in the Bible where God allows us to test Him. In all other places, we must believe, or have faith, for us to receive the promises.

If you have been having faith in your tithing and giving for prosperity, please do the following:

- Repent (change your mind).

- Ask Him to redeem your tithes and offerings that were given incorrectly.

- Remember that Father God wants to bless you.

- Now continue to give your tithes and offerings with your faith solidly in Jesus as your sole provider and the source of your prosperity.

Chapter 3

Are You Afraid To Not Tithe And Give?

If you are tithing and giving because you are afraid not to tithe and give, God cannot bless you. Can God bless anything done out of fear? What you are really afraid of is that God will not meet your needs or that you will be poor. Please think for a moment about what this kind of attitude says about your God, His love, and His fatherhood. This kind of attitude indicates that God is sitting in heaven with a big club raised, ready to smack you. It also indicates that you think God can be bribed.

If you are afraid that you will be poor, that your needs will not be met, then that is exactly what will happen to you. That may be why your tithing and giving is not working. In Job 3:25, Job said,

For what I *fear* comes upon me, and what I *dread* comes (emphasis added).

We are clearly taught, from Genesis through Revelation, that what we fear will come upon us. It has been said that phrases like "do not fear," "do not be afraid," "fear not," and "do not be anxious" appear in the Bible 366 times, one for every day of the year, including leap year.

Some dear friends of ours who grew up as Southern Baptists learned to tithe and were very prosperous. The man had the oversight of several savings and loans institutions. He and his wife were filled with the Holy Spirit and began giving more than the tithe, expecting God's hundredfold return. He started his own business and began construction of a new home.

Somewhere things began to go amiss. They lost two houses, and the business filed for bankruptcy. We helped them move to Broken Arrow, Oklahoma, to start over. The man quickly got a job and rented a house. However, within a few months, he was behind several months' rent. At times, he and his wife had only cereal or peanut butter to eat. She was sitting in our den one day when my wife asked her, "If someone gave you twenty-five dollars right now, would you tithe?" She responded, "Oh, I would be afraid not to tithe." I said, "Wow! Your tithing has really been working for you, hasn't it? Your fear is why God has not been able to bless you."

My wife felt led of the Lord to go to this woman's house five days a week, take her a little something, and pray with her until this situation was broken. It took several weeks, but the man became a vice president of a savings and loan, got a car and house at unbelievably low prices, and became part owner of a restaurant. God began to bless them the way He had been wanting to all along. Praise God!

Please, if you are tithing and giving out of fear, do the following:

- Repent.

- Ask God to change you so that you never again give out of fear.

- After you have dealt with this fear, ask God to redeem all the tithes and offerings that you gave out of fear.

- When you have done this, continue to tithe and give because you love Him.

CHAPTER 4

Are You Tithing And Giving With No Rejoicing? Are You Forced, Coerced, Or Feeling Guilty? Did You Give, Or Were You Taken?

Several years ago, a certain minister was preaching over the radio when we heard him tell how his publishing company was in real financial need. He said he was pacing in his office, telling God how his company had given much to spread the gospel. He wanted to know where the return was for the company. He related how he had published many books for various ministers who had never paid him. He told of how some came in and asked him to publish their books, and rather than miss God by not printing the books, he had published them anyway. He related some ten to twelve stories. He asked God where the hundredfold return was for all this giving. Finally, God spoke to him and said, "Why, son, you did not *give* all this. You were taken!"

Have you ever given into an offering when instead of giving, you were taken? Well, I have, but no more.

In Exodus 35:4–5, the Bible says,

> Moses spoke to all the congregation of the sons of Israel, saying, 'This is the thing which the LORD has commanded, saying, "Take from among you a contribution to the LORD; *whoever is of a willing heart*, let him bring it as the LORD's contribution: gold, silver, and bronze"' (emphasis added).

Exodus 35:21–22 says,

> Everyone *whose heart stirred him* and *everyone whose spirit moved him* came and brought the LORD's contribution. . . . Then all *whose hearts moved them*, both men and women, came and brought (emphasis added).

Additionally, verse 29 says,

> The Israelites, all the men and women, *whose heart moved them* . . . (emphasis added).

It certainly appears that God did not want gifts from those whose hearts did not move them. It is implied that they were not permitted to give if their hearts did not move them, and there was no condemnation for those who did not give.

Frankly, when ministers make an impassioned plea for money and pull it out of people who do not have a willing heart, I wonder if the ministers are not bringing a curse on their offering. It is certain that God wants gifts only from those who have willing hearts.

What was the result of the giving from those whose hearts moved them? Exodus 36:5–6 says,

> And they [the craftsmen] said to Moses, 'The people are bringing much more than enough for the construction work which the LORD commanded us to perform.' So Moses issued a command, and a proclamation was circulated throughout the camp, saying, 'Let no man or woman any longer perform work for the contributions of the sanctuary.' *Thus the people were restrained from bringing any more* (emphasis added).

Wouldn't it be wonderful to go to church and hear the pastor say, "Whoa! Folks, you are going to have to do something else with your gifts. We have so much we don't know what to do with it all." This is God's plan for the churches: that they have so much that the people would have to be restrained from giving.

King David was gathering some of the materials for the construction of the temple and in 1 Chronicles 29:6–9, the Bible says:

> Then the rulers of the fathers' households, and the princes of the tribes of Israel, and the commanders of thousands and of hundreds, with the overseers over the king's work, *offered willingly*; and for the service for the house of God they gave 5,000 talents and 10,000 darics of gold, and 10,000 talents of silver, and 10,000 talents of brass and 100,000 talents of iron. Whoever possessed precious stones gave them to the treasury of the house of the Lord, in care of Jehiel the Gershonite. Then the people *rejoiced* because they had *offered so willingly*, for they made their offering to the Lord *with a whole heart*, and King David also rejoiced greatly. (emphasis added)

Notice that when the offering is made with a willing heart, there is more than enough.

Who first tithed? In Genesis 14:18–20, we find that Abram, before he was called Abraham, was the first to tithe. Where did he get the tithe? He had just rescued Lot and the people and goods of Sodom and Gomorrah. The tithe he gave to Melchizedek came from the goods he had just taken from the enemy.

Where did the people of Israel get the goods to give for the construction of the tabernacle? They got it from their enemies, the Egyptians. Where did the people and David get the materials for the building of the temple? It was from the spoils of war taken from their enemies. Friends, we need to learn how to plunder the enemy instead of plundering fellow Christians.

In the New Testament, 2 Corinthians 9:7 says,

> Let each one do just as he has purposed in his heart; not grudgingly or under compulsion; for God loves a cheerful giver.

The word *grudgingly* in Greek means pain of mind, grief, or sorrow. The word *compulsion* means necessity, obligation, or distress. The word *cheerful* means hilarious, jumping up and down and doing twirls in the air. Notice, *you* decide when to give and how much to give—not someone else telling you what to do. This decision is made in your heart, not in your head. The heart is where the Spirit resides. Your giving must be directed by the Holy Spirit.

Dear one, if you cannot rejoice when you tithe or give, you might as well put your money back in your pocket, because there will be no blessing coming. It is true that it will aid the one you gave it to, but it will do nothing for you. You have wasted your seed. There is even a chance that your begrudged gift could be a curse to the one receiving it.

The above verse says "as he has purposed." My wife and I now pray *before* we go to church or a meeting; we ask God if we are to give, and if so, how much. We purpose in our hearts before we get there to ensure that we are being led by the Spirit. Occasionally, when we get there, a special offering may come up that we did not know about. We then pray together while sitting in the pew and get God's instructions. If we do not get specific instructions from Him, we do not give.

Since it is people or organizations that actually get what you give, what does God get? The only thing God gets from your tithing and giving is your love, honor, thanksgiving—your heart's attitude. God is more interested in your relationship with Him than He is in your giving. Your heart's attitude really speaks of the condition of your relationship with Father God.

Proverbs 3:9–10 says,

> Honor the LORD from your wealth and from the first of all your produce; so your barns will be filled with plenty [financial prosperity], and your vats will overflow with new wine [fresh revelations].

It is evident that for us to see a return on our tithes and offerings, they must be a form of honor and worship. Therefore, if you cannot rejoice or honor the Lord with the amount you are going to give, then reduce the amount to a level that will allow you to rejoice, or do not give at all.

In 2 Corinthians 8:12, the Lord says that

> if the readiness [to give] is present, it is acceptable *according to what a man has*, not according to what he does not have (emphasis added).

If you have been giving from compulsion rather than from a willing heart, consider the following:

- Confess what you feel to the Father, and ask Him to set you free so you can give with a heart full of joy.

- Ask the Father to redeem those tithes and gifts that were made when you could not and did not rejoice, and ask Him to credit them to your account now that you have repented.

CHAPTER 5

ARE YOU IN AGREEMENT WITH YOUR MATE?

Often it is either the husband or the wife who has control of the finances. Frequently, when it comes time to write the tithe check or give an offering, the one controlling the checkbook writes the check without even asking their mate. God wants to use tithes and offerings as a point where He can bring the husband and wife into agreement in the Spirit so that He can train them how to flow together in the Spirit in other matters.

The opposite of agreement is strife. Jesus said that if we were not for Him we would be against Him. In another place, He said that is someone was for Him, they would not be against Him. He said it both ways. Many ministers have taken God's Word and "read it backwards" to bring out some great truths of the Bible. Using this same principle, if you and your mate are not in agreement, then it follows that you are in strife. With God it is not possible to straddle the fence.

In James 3:16, the Bible says,

> For where jealousy and selfish ambition [in the margin it reads 'strife'] exist, there is disorder and every evil thing.

Therefore, it is important for the husband and wife to come to an agreement about how much to give, to whom to give, when to give, and how to give. I believe that God will not bless your giving if you and your mate are not in agreement.

An excellent example of the power that can be released when a husband and wife are in agreement about giving can be found in 2 Kings 4:8–37. Elisha was fed often by a Shunammite woman. She asked her husband to build a small room for him to rest. The husband agreed and built the room and outfitted it with a bed, table, chair, and lamp stand.

Elisha asked the woman what he could do for her. Being childless, she was given a son. A few years later, the son died. The woman traveled to Elisha, believing that all would be well. The son was restored to life and given back to the woman. All of this occurred because she and her husband were in agreement and gave from a willing heart to a man of God.

Therefore, when it comes time to give, husbands and wives should pray about who, when, and how much and then come together in a flowing, unforced agreement. There may be times when only one will get the exact information, but the other mate should agree willingly, joyfully, and freely. This is one way that God has of causing things to occur as He desires, both in the amount of the tithe or gift as well as in the timing. Do not give anything until you and your mate are in agreement. Notice, God is more interested in your relationship with your mate than He is in your giving.

If you have tithed or given while out of agreement with your mate, do the following:

- Repent (remember this means to change your mind).

- Make amends with your mate.

- Ask God to redeem what was given incorrectly.

CHAPTER 6

ARE YOU AND YOUR MATE ON GOOD TERMS?

It is amazing that as God began to reveal some of the reasons why our tithes and offerings were not being blessed, it became clear that God is more interested in relationships than He is in giving. He is concerned about your relationship with Him, your mate, your children, and others.

In Malachi 2:13–14, the Word of God says,

> This is another thing you do: you cover the altar of the LORD with tears, with weeping and with groaning, because *He no longer regards the offering or accepts it with favor from your hand.* Yet you say, 'For what reason?' Because the LORD has been witness between you and the wife of your youth, against whom you have dealt

treacherously, though she is your companion and your wife by covenant (emphasis added).

Notice that if you have mistreated your mate, lied, betrayed, been unfaithful, deceived, or been unfair, your giving will not be accepted by the Father. He has no regard for your offering. Therefore, if you and your mate are having marriage difficulties, take the following steps in regards to your tithes and offerings:

- Wait to give until you have been restored to fellowship with each other.

- Ask the Father to redeem the gifts given while you and your mate were out of sorts. Since the relationship of a man and his wife is similar to the relationship of Jesus and the church, start now to restore your marriage.

- If you and your mate belong to Jesus, there is no greater priority than getting your marriage on solid footing.

- Remember, God created the family four thousand years before He created the church.

CHAPTER 7

ARE YOU MEETING YOUR FAMILY'S NEEDS?

If you have been tithing and giving instead of meeting your family's basic needs of food, shelter, and clothing (I am not referring to giving your teenager a new car, overpriced designer jeans, etc.), then you are in trouble with God.

First Timothy 5:8 says,

> But if anyone does not provide for his own, and especially for those of his own household, *he has denied the faith, and is worse than an unbeliever* (emphasis added).

Remember, God created the family four thousand years before He created the church.

In Matthew 15:1–2, the Pharisees and scribes were condemning the disciples for not washing their hands in accordance with man's tradition.

In Matthew 15:3–6, Jesus answered, saying,

> And why do you yourselves transgress the commandment of God for the sake of your *tradition*? For God said, 'Honor your father and mother' [this means to take care of them], and, 'He who speaks evil of father or mother, let him be put to death.' But you say, 'Whoever says to his father or mother, "Whatever I have that would help you has been given to God," he is not to honor his father or his mother' (emphasis added)

The Living Bible says it this way in Matt. 15:5–9

> But you say, 'Even if your parents are in need, you may give their support money to the church instead.' He is not to honor his father or his mother, and thus you invalidated the word of God for the sake of your *tradition*. You hypocrites, rightly did Isaiah prophesy of you saying, 'This people honors me with their lips, but their

heart is far from me. But in vain do they worship me, *teaching as doctrines the precepts of men'* (emphasis added).

Notice that Jesus really blasted the Pharisees and scribes for following the tradition of man instead of the Word of God. Here Jesus called the people who gave to the church instead of taking care of their parents "hypocrites."

I was sharing this point in a home Bible study one night when the wife of one of the young couples attending began to cry. I asked what was wrong. The husband explained that just a few days before, he had taken the last fifty dollars they had and given it to the church. It was all the money they had to live on, to buy food for two children. He said that he had been taught that you had to pay the tithe, even if no one else got paid. It was obvious that the wife was not in agreement, that there was strife in the family, and that the wife felt betrayed and unfairly treated. He was guilty of verses 5 and 6 of Matthew 15. The children had a picture of God as a big meanie who demanded their money even if they had nothing to eat and had holes in their shoes and pants. Dear ones, God is more interested in how He appears to your children than He is in your giving. That is why He gave us 1 Timothy 5:8.

Jesus said that it would be better for a millstone to be tied around our neck and for us to be dropped into the sea than for us to cause a little one to stumble. Surely you can see what kind of picture of God your family sees when you give to the church and fail to provide for their needs, and how this could cause them to stumble.

If you have a heart's desire to give but are not able to tithe now, then start where you are, give what you can, and trust God to advance and bless you to the place where you can tithe and give.

As 2 Corinthians 8:12 says,

> For if the readiness [desire to give] is present, it is acceptable according to *what a person has*, not according to what he does not have (emphasis added).

If you have been tithing and giving instead of meeting your family's basic needs, repent.

This disagrees with much that many of us have been taught in the past. Therefore, take the following steps:

- I ask you to study the scriptures that are in this book, go before God in prayer, and get His instructions.

- I ask you to set aside all of men's traditions and teachings on tithes and offerings, including any in this book, study the Word of God, and come to your own conclusions.

- Then do as your Father God directs.

CHAPTER 8

ARE YOU TITHING AND GIVING INSTEAD OF PAYING PAST-DUE BILLS?

Are you tithing and giving to God instead of paying past-due bills? For example, if you have in your right hand past-due bills totaling a hundred dollars, and somehow you get exactly a hundred dollars placed into your left hand, should you tithe or give out of the hundred dollars you just received? Many times when we have asked people that question, they immediately respond, "Yes! I would give." This is a major reason why so many Christian people who are in need stay in need and often get in even worse financial condition.

When you have past-due bills—these are the key words: *past-due bills*—and money to pay those bills, the money you have, in a sense, is not legally yours. For example, several lawyers have told us that if you have a past-due bill in one hand

and money to pay the bill in the other hand, the person you owe could go to a judge for action. The judge would quickly take the money from you and give it to the person you owe. If, in this sense, the money is not yours but belongs to the person you owe, if some of that money is given to the Lord, the blessings on the gift go to the one who owns the gift, which is the person you owe, not you. They get the blessing, while you get deeper in debt. In fact, you are giving *stolen* money to God! The money you gave to God did not cost you anything—*it cost the person you owe*. That is why the blessing goes to them.

Luke 21:1–4 says,

> And He looked up and saw the rich putting their gifts into the treasury. And He saw a certain poor widow putting in two small copper coins. And He said, 'Truly I say to you, this poor widow put in more than all of them; for they all out of their surplus put into the offering; but she out of her poverty put in *all that she had to live on* (emphasis added).

Notice, it was all she had to live on. Her bills were paid, and this was her food money, her clothing money, etc. This was *her* money to give. This passage has often been used to illustrate how we should give. However, when this verse is taken in context, it will be realized that Jesus was not praising this widow, nor was He using her as an example of how we should give; but rather, He was giving a real live example of the error taught by the Pharisees and scribes. In the last verse of Luke 20, Jesus had stated that their *teachings* and *traditions* devoured widows' houses. There was absolutely no place in the law where everything one had to live on must be given to God. The tithes and gifts came from the increase God blessed them with.

In 2 Samuel 24, David sinned by numbering the people. God told David to choose one of three things that God would do to him for sinning. He chose a plague. Seventy thousand men died. David cried out to God that it was he who had sinned, so why punish these sheep? The plague was stopped at the threshing floor of Araunah, the Jebusite. David went there to offer a burnt offering to God.

In verses 22–25 of 2 Samuel 24, the Bible says:

> Araunah said to David, "Let my lord the king take and offer up what is good in his sight. Look, the oxen for the burnt offering, the threshing sledges and the yokes of the oxen for the wood. Everything, O king, Araunah gives to the king." And Araunah

said to the king, "May the LORD your God accept you." However, the king said to Araunah, "No, but I will surely buy it from you for a price [one translation says 'for a good price'), for I will not offer burnt offerings to the LORD my God *which cost me nothing*." So David bought the threshing floor and the oxen for fifty shekels of silver. And David built there an altar to the Lord, and offered burnt offerings and peace offerings. Thus the Lord was moved by entreaty for the land, and the plague was held back from Israel. (emphasis added)

King David paid Araunah a good price for the oxen and other items. One of the reasons he bought the oxen and other things to offer to the Lord is that he knew if he took it as a gift and offered it to God, Araunah would get the blessing. The reason is that the gift would have cost Araunah, not David, and the blessing would have gone to Araunah, not David. David wanted to give to God something that cost him. He did not want to give anything cheap to his Lord.

If money for past-due bills belongs to the person owed, and we give some of that money to God, it is considered to be stolen money.

As Malachi 1:13–14 says,

> You also say, 'My, how tiresome it is!' And you disdainfully sniff at it," says the LORD of hosts, "and you bring what was *taken by robbery*, and what is lame or sick; so you bring the offering! Should I receive that from your hand?" says the LORD. "*But cursed be the swindler* [thief] who has a male in his flock and vows it, but sacrifices a blemished animal to the LORD, for I am a great King," says the LORD of hosts, "and My name is feared among the nations (emphasis added).

Notice, if we give something stolen to God, someone else gets the blessing, and under the law, we bring a curse upon ourselves. Praise God, we are not under the law!

Also notice that God is interested in what the world thinks of Him: "My name is feared among the nations." He cares about what He looks like in the eyes of unbelievers.

This is why He said in Romans 13:8,

> Owe nothing to anyone except to love one another; for he who loves his neighbor has fulfilled the law.

God wants you to pay your bills. Can you see the picture we paint of God to the unbeliever if we tithe or give to the Lord but let the unbeliever go unpaid? Can you imagine what kind of God this makes the unbeliever think our God is, that He demands our money even if he (the unbeliever) has to do without because we will not pay our bills?

A few years ago, a good Christian man in Tulsa was forced into bankruptcy. He petitioned the court to allow him to continue to tithe. The judge decreed, "Absolutely not! Pay your creditors!" This news made all the TV stations and newspapers, and they greatly ridiculed the man. At first, I thought that he was right in wanting to continue to tithe. However, as the Lord began to reveal these truths, I saw that the judge was right and that religion (tradition) was wrong. After all, it was religion (tradition) that put Jesus to death on the cross.

Right now, the unbelievers see the church as takers, not givers. In the recent scandals that have hit televangelism, did you notice it was not the issue of sex that the media really addressed, but the financial excesses, extravagances, and donations? *It was the money issue!* The Lord wants the world to see the church as givers, not takers.

I am sure that we can think of hundreds of churches where we can go to find peace with God, get healed, get delivered, and get saved and filled with the Holy Spirit. How many churches do you know where an average Christian with a financial need can go and expect to see God move supernaturally and have that financial need met? Jesus died for our prosperity just as surely as He died to give us a home in heaven. In Acts 2:43–47 and Acts 4:32–37, the Bible tells how members of the church sold land and houses and brought the proceeds to the apostles, and there was no one in the church who had a financial need (Acts 4:34). Years later Paul took an offering from the many Gentile churches to Jerusalem for the poor saints in the Jerusalem church (Rom. 15:26). It is also important to remember that in the Year of Jubilee, houses and lands were returned to the original owners in accordance with Jewish law.

You have probably heard testimonies from people where God told them to give the rent money, telephone money, or car-note money to Him, and then He quickly caused the increase to come forth. Notice, if the Spirit of God tells you to do something and you obey, it will always work. However, do you know someone who heard such a testimony and tried to do the same thing "because God is not a respecter of persons," but it did not work for them, and they got into trouble instead? Trying to do what God told someone else to do, when God did not tell you to do it, can cause tremendous damage, even death. For example, God told the people of Israel to walk through the Red Sea on dry land, and they did. However, He did not tell the Egyptians to do that; they tried to do what the Jews did, and every one of them perished in the sea. Trying to live someone else's testimony can be fatal.

Are you in such a financial condition that your family would have to go without basic needs being met and people you owe would have to go unpaid if you tithed or gave to the Lord? God would rather you meet those needs first, then give to Him something that costs *you*, not your family or those you owe.

A young couple came to us for help with their finances. We sat down with them and worked out a budget, which included tithing and giving. They had never heard of a budget or how to set up one. We took about three months of bank records and determined an average amount spent for food, utilities, gasoline, etc., along with payments that were owed every month. When we totaled these fixed expenses, the husband's income was not sufficient to meet their basic needs.

We went to the bank to obtain a bill-consolidation loan to reduce their monthly notes. This effort failed. We next considered going to each creditor and asking them to reduce the monthly notes. After prayer, we decided not to do that. After exhausting all other possibilities, we told the couple that they had no money to give to the Lord and that they would have to stop tithing. The man went into orbit. He had been taught to tithe—regardless. He said that he had to give something to God—or bust.

We asked him how much he spent for lunch each day. He said about $2.50. We suggested that he fast as many of his lunches as he wanted and give that money to God, because it was his money to live on. However, I warned him not to take bill money or money for the basic needs of his family to give to the Lord. The man was obedient to do as he was told. In less than one year, he was completely out of debt and able to tithe again. A short time later, someone gave them a car—paid for, free and clear.

If you ever find yourself in a similar condition as this young couple and feel you must give to the Lord, consider a bill-consolidation loan to reduce your payments. Or you might go to each of your creditors and ask them to work with you as you work your way out of debt. This might free up some cash to allow you to give without falling into the trap discussed in this chapter.

Remember, as 2 Corinthians 8:12 says,

> For if the readiness is present, it is acceptable according to *what a man has*, not according to *what he does not have* (emphasis added).

Brothers and sisters, if you have been guilty of giving bill money to God, please do the following:

- Repent.

- Start today to give correctly what is yours to give.

- Start where you are.

- Give what you can.

- If you are unable to give to God and begin to feel guilty about this, recognize that it is the devil accusing you, not God. There is no condemnation for those who are in Christ Jesus.

- If you are in the position where you are not able to give, buy only the basic necessities of life. Do not buy anything else until you pay off enough of your debts that you can give to the Lord because you love Him, not out of need, guilt, or fear.

CHAPTER 9

ARE YOU GIVING BECAUSE YOU SAW A NEED?

It is good to give to those in need. However, there are some things we need to know when we start giving to individuals. For example, have you ever felt the Lord wanted you to tell someone about Him, so you went right then and told that person about Jesus and got your tail feathers burned? What happened?

Psalm 19:13 says,

> Also keep back Your servant from *presumptuous* sins; let them not rule over me; then I will be blameless, and I shall be acquitted of great transgression.

This is one of the biggest forgivable sins that a Christian can commit. To answer the question of what happened, the answer is that we committed the sin of presumption. We presumed that the Lord meant for us to go tell that person right then. We should have prayed and asked, "Lord, when do I go tell them?" We should then have asked, "Lord, how do I tell them, and what do I tell them?"

There may have been times that we had extra money, and we saw a need. Since we had extra and saw the need, we may have presumed that we were to meet the need. James 2:14–18 says the following:

> What use is it, my brethren, if a man says he has faith, but he has no works? Can that faith save him? If a *brother* or *sister* is without clothing and in need of daily food, and one of you says to them, "Go in peace, be warmed and be filled," and yet you do not give them what is necessary for their body, what use is that? Even so faith, if it has no works, is dead, being by itself.
>
> But someone may well say, "You have faith, and I have works; show me your faith without the works, and I will show you my faith by my works." (emphasis added)

The Bible says that if we see a *brother* or *sister* naked or hungry, we do not need to pray about this; we are to meet the need. The church meeting the needs of its own body should be one of the forces that draw the world to Jesus.

However, if the brother or sister is not naked or hungry, it is a different story. First John 3:17–18 tells us,

> Whoever has the world's goods, and beholds his *brother* in need and closes *his heart* against him, how does the love of God abide in him? Little children, let us not love with work or with tongue, but in deed and truth (emphasis added)

Notice again that Scripture says a "brother." It also says that if you have the ability to meet the need, do not close your heart; it does not say "pocketbook." This means that we are to go to the Lord and ask Jesus what we should do about the need. The heart is where the Spirit is—it is not the mind. If we see someone in need and refuse to pray about it, then our faith is useless. Here it requires much prayer to be sure that we have the will of the Father.

In 2 Thessalonians 3:10, God's Word says,

> For even when we were with you, we used to give you this order: if anyone will not work, neither let him eat.

It does not say that the person must be working for money; he just has to be working. Our youngest son, Daryl, felt led of the Lord to do volunteer work for two ministries in Tulsa. He worked for one ministry for three months and the other one for six months without being paid by the ministry. However, because he worked just like an employee—faithful, on time, etc.—we saw our Father God meet all his financial needs, provide gas for his car, money for dates, etc. This really blessed us to see the faithfulness of Father God.

Several years ago in a church where we were going, one of the elders and another couple asked the church for prayer and financial assistance. At this time, my wife and I had extra money and could have met both of their needs. We began seeking the Lord about how much we should give to these brothers. Neither one of us could get an amount from the Lord.

After about three weeks, with them asking at each church service for prayer, thoughts began to come to us such as "If you see your brother in need and do nothing, what good is your faith?" and "Him that knoweth to do good and doeth it not, to him it is sin." We were really being badgered by the Word.

I went to the pastor and explained to him what had been happening. I wanted him to pray with us so we could hear God. When I finished, he said, "Oh, praise God! Brother, you have been obedient to God *not to give*." I was floored and asked him to explain. He said that he had watched God take eight years to get the elder into this position so He could teach him how to use his finances correctly. The other couple wasted their money. They would buy their children every conceivable toy possible — three-wheel motorcycles, etc. — instead of paying their bills. The pastor said that if we had not been patient to get instructions from God and obedient to God to not give, we would have messed up years of God's work in their lives.

Later the Lord spoke to me and said, "Son, I have called you and your wife to be givers. But if your giving begins to mess up others' lives and what I am doing in their lives, I will see to it that you do not have money to mess up what I am doing." Believe me, this got my undivided attention. You see, when we give, it is important to give the correct amount to the penny at the right time to the right person, or our giving may well be wasted, with no blessing. The Father is interested in the timing of the gift just as much as He is interested in the amount. It is critical that we be obedient and be led by the Holy Spirit when we tithe and give.

In Matthew 25:31–40, Jesus said:

> But when the Son of Man comes in His glory and all the angels with Him, then He will sit on His glorious throne. And all the nations will be gathered before Him; and He will separate them from one another, as the shepherd separates the sheep from the goats; and He will put the sheep on His right, and the goats on the left. Then the King will say to those on His right, "Come, you who are blessed of My Father, inherit the kingdom prepared for you from the foundation of the world. For I was hungry, and you gave Me something to eat; I was thirsty, and you gave Me drink; I was a stranger, and you invited Me in; naked, and you clothed Me; I was sick, and you visited Me; I was in prison, and you came to Me." Then the righteous will answer Him, saying, "Lord, when did we see You hungry, and feed You, or thirsty, and give You something to drink? And when did we see You a stranger, and invite You in, or naked,

and clothe You? When did we see You sick, or in prison, and come to You?" The King will answer and say to them, "Truly I say to you, *to the extent that you did it to one of these brothers of mine, even the least of them, you did it to Me.*" (emphasis added)

Notice that in this judgment, we will be judged for what we did for our brothers and sisters in Jesus—not how much we gave to churches or ministries, not how many buildings we built, not how many chairs we bought, and not how many choir robes we purchased. We will be judged by what we did for even the least of them. The goats in verses 41–46 were condemned because they did not do anything for Jesus' "least of them." (Please keep this chapter in mind when you read and study chapter 12).

- Remember, it is important to tithe and give.

- However, if we really want to see God's blessings, we must be led by the Spirit when we tithe and give.

CHAPTER 10

DOES SOMEONE HAVE SOMETHING AGAINST YOU?

If you know that a brother or sister in the Lord has something against you, you might as well not give until you make an attempt to restore them to fellowship. In Matthew 5:23–24, Jesus said,

> If therefore you are presenting your offering at the altar, and there remember that your brother has something against you, leave your offering there before the altar, and go your way. First be reconciled to you brother, and then come and present your offering.

For us to be blessed in our tithes and offerings, God wants us to be walking in love with our brothers and sisters. He wants them to be walking in love with us. Failure to attempt to restore our brother short-circuits the blessing on our giving. Again, God is more interested in relationships than He is in our giving. Have you noticed how many of the chapters in this book deal with relationships?

We should make every effort to restore ourselves with those who have something against us. I do believe that after we have done everything possible, if the brother will not be restored, we are free to give and it will be blessed. The problem is now his problem only, and he will have to resolve that with God.

Therefore, consider the following steps:

- If you know there are brothers and sisters who have sinned against you, suspend your giving and set your tithes and offerings aside until you make every effort to restore the relationship.

- Ask the Holy Spirit to reveal to you if there are present problems that you know nothing about.

- Spend time in prayer and fasting

- Get others to agree with you that the fellowship with those who have something against you will be restored.

- Matthew 18:12–35 is all about restoring a brother or sister to fellowship. This includes Matthew 18:19, which is the prayer of agreement.

- After you have made the attempt to restore these relationships, bring your tithes and offerings to the Lord, and just watch for His blessings to be poured out upon you.

CHAPTER 11

DO YOU HAVE UNFORGIVENESS IN YOUR HEART?

Harboring unforgiveness in your heart toward anyone for any reason will rob you of almost everything Jesus died to give you except your home in heaven. Unforgiveness will totally shut off God's prosperity to you. As you remember, Job had three "friends" who kept beating him over the head with the Word while he was in agony. In Job 26:4, Job was so angry with them that he questioned the spirit that was in them. In Job 42:7–9, God told these three friends to go to Job and get him to pray for them, or God Himself would deal with them. Job was madder than a wet hen with them at the time. God was expressing His faith in Job when He told them to get Job to pray for them.

Job 42:10 says,

> And the Lord restored the fortunes of Job *when he prayed for his friends*, and the Lord increased all that Job had twofold (emphasis added).

Brothers and sisters, if Job had not forgiven those three friends, he would have died on the ash heap, full of sores. But he did forgive them. You cannot really pray for someone and be harboring unforgiveness in your heart toward them.

In Bible studies, we have often asked what Luke 6:38 says. The first word is "give." Every time, many could quote the verse. We then asked what Luke 6:37 says. Only one person in all those times could quote that verse.

Luke 6:38 says,

> Give, and it will be given to you. They will pour into your lap a good measure—pressed down, shaken together, and running over. For by your standard of measure it will be measured to you in return.

Notice, however, that the good measure, the pressing down, and the running over are dependent on Luke 6:37, which says,

> Do not judge and you will not be judged; and do not condemn, and you will not be condemned; pardon [forgive], and you will be pardoned [forgiven].

Unforgiveness will cost you your fellowship with the Father, Jesus, and the Holy Spirit (see Matthew 6:8–15, especially verses 14–15). It will cost you your health (see Matthew 18:21–35, especially verses 34–35) and your prosperity (Job 42:10; Luke 6:37–38), and your faith will not work (see Mark 11:22–26, especially verses 25–26, and Galatians 5:6). We simply cannot afford resentment, hard feelings, animosity, or unforgiveness. We just cannot afford the "pleasure" of harboring those feelings.

The reason so many of us get trapped in unforgiveness is because of the anger we feel or the emotions we experience when we remember the event that hurt us so deeply. The secret of walking in forgiveness is found in Matthew 18:35. That verse says,

> So shall My heavenly Father also do to you, if each of you does not forgive his brother *from your heart* (emphasis added).

Although we have forgiven in the past, when the remembrance comes up and the rage with it, we assume that we have not forgiven. Notice that forgiveness comes from the heart—not the head, not the emotions, and not the feelings. It is with our spirit man, the new man, that we *choose* to forgive. We make the choice with our heart, and it becomes real.

The Lord showed us that our lives are like a train. The engine is the will, and the caboose is the emotions. Many of us run around with our train in reverse; what we feel is what we will. For example if we get up in the morning feeling great, we will to have a great day. If we arise feeling bad, we will to have a miserable day. However, when we will something different from what our emotions are feeling, the train stops.

We must choose to forgive instead of living in unforgiveness. When we do, the train stops and begins to go forward instead of in reverse, heading toward forgiveness. The caboose is still feeling the hate, hostility, or anger. The engine may move several hundred feet down the track, taking the slack out of the couplings between the cars, before the caboose ever detects that the train is going the other way. Then the train has to travel its entire length before the caboose reaches the same spot on the tracks where the engine was when the engine willed to forgive.

What I am saying is this: you can will, or choose, to forgive from your heart even while you are red in the face, with your fists and teeth clenched, and the forgiveness will be as real as Jesus. Also, it will take time for you to feel the forgiveness you chose to make in your heart. The deeper the hurt, the longer the train, and the longer it may take for you to feel the forgiveness that has come from your heart.

Please consider the following:

- Let the Holy Spirit search your heart to find if there is any unforgiveness toward anyone for any reason (see 1 Corinthians 4:3–5).

- If He shows you any wrong, quickly repent and choose to forgive from your heart.

- You may need to forgive others.

- You may also need to forgive yourself.

- If you have ever said or thought these words, "God, why did You do that to me?" or "God, why did You let that happen to me?" you have hardness in your heart towards God. Job did (see Job 23:1–7). However, in Job 42:1–6, Job repented.

- This is what you must do: repent. God can do no wrong.

- Any tithing or giving that you do while your heart has unforgiveness in it towards anyone for anything will void the blessing that God wants you to have.

- God is more concerned about your relationships than He is about your giving.

- I believe that unforgiveness is the biggest stumbling block there is in a Christian's life. Please take care of this problem.

- Then continue to tithe and give as the Lord directs so that He can bless you.

CHAPTER 12

ARE YOU TITHING AND GIVING WITHOUT GETTING GOD'S INSTRUCTIONS ABOUT WHERE IT SHOULD GO?

Do you and your mate pray and get God's direction each time before you tithe or give? Do you automatically tithe or give to a particular church or organization without asking God what He wants? I was taught that all of the tithe went to the church where I belonged and that I did not have to pray about it. I was taught that the tithe was the first thing you paid, regardless. I was in such bondage to these teachings that when I received a paycheck and deposited it in the bank, the next check I wrote had to be the tithe check.

Could God tell you to give your tithe to an unbeliever? Could God tell you to spend the tithe on your family? Could God tell you to give the tithe to a widow or an orphan? Could God, from the Bible, tell you to do these things? Is there Scripture to back up these things?

Let me share some scriptures with you that you may not have noticed before. Deuteronomy 14:22–29 says:

> You shall surely tithe all the *produce* from what you sow, which comes out of the field every year. You shall eat in the presence of the Lord your God, *at the place where He chooses* to establish His name, the tithe of your grain, your new wine, your oil, and the firstborn of your herd and your flock, in order that you may learn to fear the LORD your God always. If the distance is so great for you that you are not able to bring the tithe, since the place where *the LORD your God chooses* to set His name is too far away from you when the LORD your God blesses you, then you shall exchange it for money, and bind the money in your hand and go to the place which *the LORD your God chooses*. You may spend the money for *whatever your heart desires* . . .; and there you shall eat in the presence of the LORD your God and rejoice, you and your household. Also you shall not neglect

the Levite who is in your town, for he has no portion or inheritance among you.

At the end of every third year you shall bring out all the tithe of your produce in that year, and shall deposit it in your town. The Levite, because he has no portion or inheritance among you, and the alien [unbeliever], the orphan and the widow who are in your town, shall come and eat and be satisfied, in order that the LORD your God may bless you in all the work of your hand which you do.

For parallel passages, see Deuteronomy 12:7, 12; 26:12.

Notice that three times in the passage in Deuteronomy 14, God says to take the tithe to the place He chooses. This means that we had better find the place He chooses if we want our tithing and giving to be blessed. That place became the temple in Jerusalem. However, one-third of the time, that place was their own town (v. 29). If the temple in Jerusalem represents our local church, then by law it gets only two-thirds of the tithe, and what then is the local storehouse? If the local storehouse represents our local church, then our local church by law should get only one-third of the tithes, and what then is the temple in Jerusalem?

The storehouse referred to in Malachi 3:10, which storehouse is it: the one in Jerusalem or the local storehouse? There was a storehouse in almost every town in Israel. This raises some very real questions, doesn't it? To be truthful, I do not have the answers to these questions either. But you see, we are no longer under the law, and the easy way out of this is to ask God where He chooses when we give every time. Then get His instructions.

Could God tell you to spend the tithe on your own family? Yes (v. 26). I have been tithing since I was six years old, but only twice in my life has the Father told me to spend the tithe on my family. At least I am now open to hear Him tell me to do this. Look at the last few lines of verse 29. If we want the works of our hands to be blessed, we must give as He directs. In other words, we must be led by the Spirit when we tithe and give.

Let us bring this into balance. Remember, the tithe was a full year's worth of produce. It would be impossible for one family to eat the entire tithe. That is why there was plenty for the Levites in the towns. Who were the Levites? They were the priests, right? Wrong! The priests had to be direct descendants from Aaron. The Levites were the singers, musicians, ushers, gatekeepers, carriers of the ark, etc. They were the ministry of helps. Numbers 18:21 says,

> To the sons of Levi, behold, I have given all the tithe in Israel for an inheritance, in return for their service which they perform, *the service of the tent of meeting* (emphasis added).

Also see Nehemiah 10:37 and 13:10–13.

Could God tell you to give the tithe to an unbeliever, the lost fellow down the street who lost his job three months ago? Yes—look at verse 29. The alien is the unbeliever. God could tell you to do this by law one-third of the time.

What about the widow and the orphan? Yes—verse 29, one-third of the time.

In Galatians 6:6–10, the Bible says:

> And let the one who is taught the word share all good things with him who teaches. Do not be deceived, God is not mocked; for whatever a man sows, this he will also reap. For the one who sows to his own flesh shall from the flesh reap corruption, but the one who sows to the Spirit shall from the Spirit reap eternal life. Let us not lose heart in doing good, for in due time we shall

reap if we do not grow weary. So then, while we have opportunity, let us *do good to all men*, and *especially to those who are of the household of faith*. (emphasis added)

Tithing and giving as the Lord directs is what brings the blessing on the works of our hands.

How did we get into this mess with our giving? I am not sure, but I think that when we stopped bringing produce, cattle, and sheep and started bringing money, we began to get off track. Tithes were always food. You cannot build buildings with food; you cannot pay utilities with food, and you cannot pay staff with food. The only thing you can do with food is feed people—meet the needs of people, especially those in the ministry.

Was Moses' tabernacle built from tithes or from offerings? Was the temple built from tithes or from offerings? They were both built from offerings.

In 1 Corinthians 9:1–15, and 1 Timothy 5:17–18, Paul teaches us that ministers have the right to derive their livelihood from those who receive their ministry. Additionally, Ephesians 4:11–13 says,

> And He gave some as apostles, and some prophets, and some evangelists, and some pastors and teachers, for the equipping of the saints for the work of service, to the building up of the body of Christ; until we all attain to the unity of the faith, and of the knowledge of the Son of God, to a mature man, to the measure of the stature which belongs to the fullness of Christ.

We need input from all five ministry offices if we are ever going to be and do what the Father wants of us. Generally, the only one of the five offices that is getting funded by the body of Christ is the pastor. Many of the others have to start churches to generate the funds to do what God has called them to do. God did not call them to pastor a church. They are not equipped for that ministry, and it is a disgrace to the church of the living God for this to happen. The main reason this is happening is that the church has not been free to be led by the Holy Spirit in the giving of their tithes and offerings.

Paul wrote several epistles in which he talked of a gift that was being taken to Jerusalem. What was the purpose of the gift? Was it to build a new church building. No! Was it to pay utilities. No! Was it to buy new choir robes, No! It was for the needy saints—all of them.

As Romans 15:26 says,

> For Macedonia and Achaia have been pleased to make a contribution for *the poor among the saints* in Jerusalem (emphasis added).

Please review Chapter 9.

Brothers and sisters in Jesus, if we want to be blessed in our tithing and giving, then we must be led by the Holy Spirit when we tithe and give—not by the traditions of man. If we are not led by the Holy Spirit when we tithe and give, then our tithing and giving is a work of the flesh, and God cannot bless it.

In the New Testament, we can be one of four things to God. We can be a slave, a servant, a friend, or a son. The choice is ours. Remember when Jesus told His disciples that He no longer called them servants, but friends. Wow, being a friend of God must be fantastic. Well, it is, but being a son is the best. Slaves, servants, and friends do not participate in the inheritance of the Father.

John 1:12 says,

> But as many as received Him, to them He gave the *right* to become children of God, even to those who believe in His name (emphasis added).

Notice that He gave us the right to be sons. Have you exercised your right to be a son of God?

If we are born again, then we are the sons of God. However, were you aware that even though we are sons, we still might not participate in the inheritance?

Galatians 4:1–2 says,

> Now I say, as long as the heir is a child [immature child], *he does not differ at all from a slave* although he is owner of everything, but he is under guardians and managers until the date set by the Father (emphasis added).

You may have noticed that when you were first born again, you were blessed when you followed men (guardians and managers). However, now you are not blessed as you once were, although you are still tithing and giving as you always did.

Good news! You have reached the date set by the Father and are no longer under guardians or managers (men). If you are still following men instead of being led by the Spirit, that may be why tithing and giving has not been working for you.

What is the requirement to be a mature son so that we can participate in the inheritance that God has for us? Romans 5:14 says,

> For *all who are being led by the Spirit of God*, these are sons [mature sons] of God (emphasis added).

Therefore, if we want to participate in our Father's inheritance, we must be led by the Spirit of God, not only in our tithing and giving, but in every area of our lives.

Finally, under the old covenant, God's people had to keep one day a week holy to the Lord. The other six days, they could do as they pleased. However, under the new covenant, which has far greater and more precious promises, we have to keep every day holy to the Lord. Also, under the old covenant, one-tenth of our goods, a tithe, belonged to the Lord. Under the new covenant, would you like to guess how much of our goods belong to the Lord? It is all His! Why? Because when we were born again, our old man, old self, old nature, died. The only thing alive in us now is Jesus. Therefore, since the only thing in us that is alive is Jesus, then all we possess is His.

Dear ones, we have a responsibility to seek God about how we spend every cent that comes into our hands—not just 10 percent, but all of it. We should get His direction when we buy cars, houses, groceries, make investments, or do anything else. This is walking in the Spirit. This is being a mature son of the Father. When we come to the place in our lives that we are led by the Spirit in our finances, then He can trust the wealth of the world into our hands because He knows, and we know, that the wealth will be distributed as He wills.

Consider the following:

- I exhort you to apply every chapter of this book to your lives.

- Ask and allow the Holy Spirit to show you if and where you have been missing it.

- Repent and make whatever adjustments the Lord asks of you.

- Then be led by the Spirit every time you tithe or give.

The Secret to Effective Tithes and Offerings

- Take a moment right now to pray about this.

- Ask the Holy Spirit to remind you of any parts of this book that touched your heart of hearts.

- Ask how you should respond.

- Repent, if necessary.

- Give this book to others who may be struggling financially.

- I know the Lord, by His Holy Spirit, will lead you in how you should tithe and give in the future, starting today.

- And please do let us know if this book has helped or blessed you. God bless you as you apply His Word to your life.

A Word To Ministers, Elders, Deacons, Board Members, And Businessmen

Today there are many ministries, churches, and businesses that are in financial trouble. I humbly submit this for your consideration: if you are in financial trouble, could it be that you are reaping what you have been sowing? Many ministries and businesses are paying their staff minimum wages or the very least that they can get by with. This is sowing seeds of poverty in your people, and you will reap a harvest of poverty in your ministry or business. In my opinion, our staffs should not be able to do the same work for someone in the world (who does not know Jesus) for more money than they can make working for us who know the Lord. God is not stingy with us. Why then are we stingy with our people?

Maybe you have been tithing from your ministry or business into other ministries. Do you really think that God will overlook how you treat your people and bless your giving? If you are an elder, deacon, board member, or businessman who sets the wages of the staff, you are in a very important position before God. I ask you to prayerfully seek God about the wages of your people. If you want to be walking in plenty, then you must sow seeds of plenty in your people. There are ministers and businessmen who have fine clothes, a big car, and a large home while their staff members struggle to just get by. This is a disgrace before God. The shepherd is to take care of the sheep, not the other way around.

James 5:4 says,

> Behold the *pay* of the laborers who mowed your fields and which has been withheld by you, cries out against you; and the outcry of those who did the harvesting has reached the ears of the Lord of Sabaoth (emphasis added).

Notice first that the *pay* cries out against you. Even if the worker does not cry out, his pay will cry out to God. Then second, the worker cries out. If your staff is crying out against you, can you see that there is strife in your camp? Where there is strife, there is every evil work. Can God bless your ministry or business as He would like to bless you? Read the verse carefully. Does not the "mower of the fields" and "harvesters" sound like the staff of a ministry or business?

There was a ministry that paid its crusade director so very little that he lost his home. The director did not make enough to meet his house note. I suggested that he look for another job, but he would not do that. He said that God wanted him there, and he would be obedient to God—period. That ministry no longer exists because it went under financially. The crusade director then became the crusade director for another ministry in Texas. One day a lady walked up to him and gave him a key. It was the key to the front door of a very nice, large house. It was his, free and clear. Praise God! The Lord more than made up for the home he lost and rewarded him for his faithfulness.

There are two things I saw that brought prosperity to my business in a much greater way. The first was when I started giving my wife money that was her very own to spend any way she wanted with no strings attached. The second was when I hired my first employee. At that time, you could hire typists all over town for five dollars an hour. Her starting wage was six dollars an hour. In less than two years, she was making eight dollars an hour. I have experienced the results of planting seeds of plenty. I have also seen the results of planting seeds of poverty.

We need to repent on our faces before God for the injustices that we have done to our staffs. We need to be planting seeds of plenty in our staffs instead of seeds of poverty, because whatever we sow, that shall we also reap.

About The Authors

Teddy and Elaine Pledger received Jesus as their Savior when they were very young. Teddy was six years of age, and Elaine was eight. They were married in 1960 and have two married sons, four grandchildren, and one great-grandchild.

Teddy and Elaine have lived for Jesus and tithed all their lives. While in their thirties, Jesus became their Lord, and shortly afterward, they were filled with the Holy Spirit. They are exhorters and teach the Word when given the opportunity. They also counsel people as the Lord directs when the need arises.

Mr. Pledger is president of AGAPÉ Incorporated, a consulting firm and crude-oil producer. He spends most of his time teaching people around the world how to make better completions and maximize oil-and-gas production and sales. Mrs. Pledger has been a homemaker all of her married life and greatly enjoys her grandchildren and great grand child. She is a prayer warrior and seeks the Lord daily for His plan and His purpose.

Our contact information is tpledger2@cox.net and epledger2@cox.net.